REDEFINE, REALIGN
AND
REDESIGN YOUR LIFE
FROM THE
INSIDE OUT

S. Yvon Harper

Connect with the WAIT! Book Author

Dedication

"W.A.I.T!" is dedicated to every person who faces the fear of moving forward, fights the fear of staying the same, or struggles with the fear of success.

I dedicate this book to every person who is ready to reach towards the promise of victory, because they have invested in the journey.

Dearest Jeri ♡

There are no words ♡ NONE to express
my love, gratitude and heart for all
you have been in my life for. God
truly answered my prayer when He
sent you into my life. Can't wait
for the rest of our adventure together.
The

Best Is
Yet To Come

Abundance & Love Always
S. Yvon Jayse
AKA
Stephanie ♡

Acknowledgements

To My:

- Faithful God, may I always slow down to "W.A.I.T!" for your divine direction in all I do. Beep! Beep!

- Husband, Timothy, who faithfully and affectionately walked with me through the process to "W.A.I.T!".

- Children, Ryan, Patricia, Charisma and Giovanni, who are in the process of learning to "W.A.I.T!". Your efforts will bring you great success.

- Parents, Freddie and Mary McQueen and the late Ophelia Harper, your wisdom has inspired me to strive to walk with giants!

- Dearest friend, Jeri Murphy, for the countless hours of help to refine my words and push forward the vision of "W.A.I.T!". Thank you for always being an open ear.

- Pastors, Frederick L. and Vanessa L. McQueen, and the entire Sanctuary Covenant Christian Fellowship family who spoke life into "W.A.I.T!".

- Family and friends for their endless support...you already know who you are. Much gratitude and a heartfelt "thank you!" to each of you.

What People Are Saying About W.A.I.T!

"Any time we can become aware of our thoughts, and beliefs, and can come off of "auto-pilot", we are automatically on the path to greater success. Yvon's book is a great catalyst to helping you form belief systems that will create the life you truly want. I particularly enjoyed the thoughtful Selah moments that started each chapter."

Jan Janzen
Author, Coach and Speaker
Author of *Devil with a Briefcase*
www.janjanzen.com

"To get the right answer we must ask the right question! S. Yvon Harper is asking the right question. The Bible says,

For as a man thinketh in his heart, so is he.

Yvon writes about identifying and addressing areas of your thought life that harbor defeat and failure. She shows us how to victoriously conquer these undesirable thoughts, which when eliminated serve to then enrich our life starting from the inside out. I support her achievement and the great effort it must have taken to produce this book."

Dan T. Cathy
President and Chief Operating Officer
Chick-fil-A, Inc.

"Two things stand out in Yvon Harper's WAIT: the clarity of the writing, and the strong sense of integrity. This is a book you can turn to whenever you need a reality check on your finances, your goals, and your dreams."

Shel Horowitz
Author/co-author of eight books including
Guerrilla Marketing Goes Green: Winning Strategies to Improve Your Profits and Your Planet
www.shelhorowitz.com

"This is a must read for those who are realizing that life is a marathon and not a sprint and need some assistance with their self motivation and training. Yvon has taken the complexities of life's journey and broken the steps into manageable pieces with an outcome of practical and spiritual results."

Karen Bankston, PhD, MSN, FACHE
University of Cincinnati
Associate Dean Clinical Practice
Partnership and Community Engagement

Table Of Contents

Table Of Contents

Table Of Contents

Redefine, Realign

And

Redesign your life

From The

Inside Out

INTRODUCTION

Setting the Stage for Discovery

A Selah Moment

"The most notable impact on what we do, become, or accomplish in life stems from what is happening in our thought life."

— S. Yvon Harper

Changing Your Cognitive State of Mind

It has been said that the greatest impact on what we do, become or accomplish in life stems from what is happening inside of us, most specifically, from the activity inside the corridors of our mind. Our cognitive state of mind, if not given proper attention, can sabotage critical areas of our life. Subconsciously, each thought, idea, or mental image creates a powerful opportunity for us to respond. The ripple affect of these responses often determine the ultimate successes or disappointments of our lives.

A Selah Moment

Pause for a moment to reflect on the above statement, which I refer to as a *"Selah Moment"*. "Selah" is a Hebrew term that means to reflect, pause, or meditate on a point of reference or wisdom. As you continue to read, you will find opportunities to "Selah" before beginning each chapter.

A Selah Moment

"An individual who fails to stop, recognize, and address negative thought patterns will never fully realize the success of reaching or sustaining their desired life goals."

— S. Yvon Harper

Why Wait?

Have you been frustrated with challenges as you seek to achieve financial freedom? Overwhelmed in your efforts to improve your relationships? Do you feel discouraged by unsuccessful attempts to accomplish your desired personal goals? Most people desire and strive to have success in not only these areas, but in every area of their lives. Many times, however, the struggle is not with their desire, but in finding the steps to ensure success.

Allow me to challenge you to examine the reality that your subliminal thoughts may be at the root of the struggle. That is why "W.A.I.T! – What Am I Thinking" was written.

"W.A.I.T!" is designed to provide you with a 10 Step program that can permanently change your life. Best of all, the action starts from the inside out, because it is the internal belief system that will be impacted.

The 10 Steps of "W.A.I.T!" are empowering as they enable success on every level, whether it is in finance, relationships, personal goals or any other areas in your life.

Be mindful that when it comes to change, the battle begins and ends in the mind. Equipped with this knowledge of the 10 Step process from "W.A.I.T!" your personal answer to "What Am I Thinking?" becomes more powerful. It is more than a mere rhetorical statement. It comes with the responsibility to be on guard for whatever is presented before the gates of your mind. Therefore, stand guard! Be meticulously aware so no unchallenged thought slips through your cognitive gates without being duly worthy to proceed.

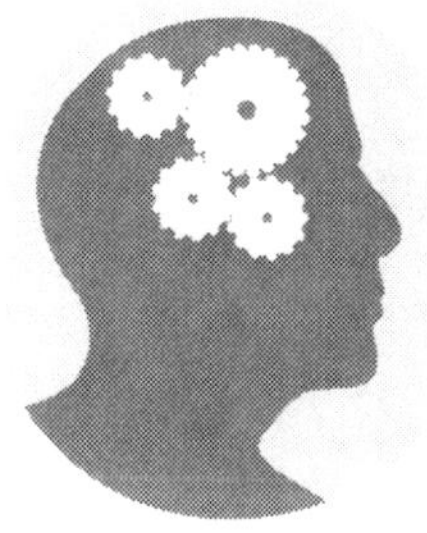

Discovery Exercises

Discovery Exercises are placed throughout "W.A.I.T!" to challenge your thought process. These Discovery Exercises will position you to intimately evaluate your current cognitive responses and help you to redefine, realign, and redesign them. Finally, Discovery Exercises help you create the new reality you desire and with that reality you are now positioned to begin the process by completing the Discovery Exercises, starting on the next page.

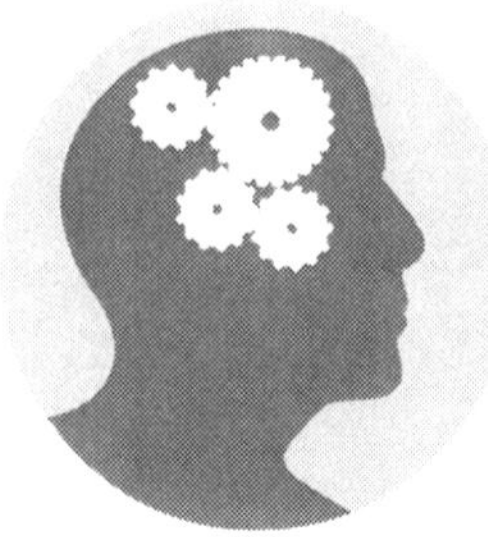

Discovery Exercise:
Why Wait?

A When you began this study what were your initial thoughts about change? Be descriptive. Were they positive, hopeful, negative, doubtful?

B Did you identify a particular thought area that you would like to examine or change? If so, what subject area did you choose to address? (Financial, personal, relationships, spiritual, etc.)

How do you intend to use the information that you receive and learn through this study? Do you intend to put it immediately into practice?

____

____

____

____

____

____

____

____

____

____

____

D In the past have you contemplated the need for change, but failed to act on it? Why?

____

____

____

____

____

____

____

____

____

____

____

E On a scale of 1 to 5 *(1=Low, 5=High)*, how serious are you about changing your thoughts and beliefs to achieve the tangible success you desire?

____

____

____

____

____

____

____

____

____

____

Your answers to these questions will give you greater insight into your cognitive thoughts today. It may surprise you to learn that as you answer the questions throughout this book they reveal the correlation between your thoughts and actions.

As you invest time to reflect and honestly answer the questions, expect to uncover patterns in how you think and respond to new ideas that challenge your established belief system.

The correlation you discover through this process is an important step. It sets the stage for you to develop and put in place milestones that gauge your progress during this journey. It also opens up your mind to new ideas. You will find yourself forming, considering, and implementing new thoughts without subliminal resistance. More importantly, you will discover how to control your actions by harnessing the power of your thoughts.

REDEFINE, REALIGN
AND
REDESIGN YOUR LIFE
FROM THE
INSIDE OUT

CHAPTER ONE

The Cost of Choosing to Change

A Selah Moment

"Your commitment to change and achieve success is one of the most powerful tools in your personal arsenal."

— *S. Yvon Harper*

Belief Systems

Generally, your belief system is rooted in what you have chosen to accept or believe, or what has been taught to you about any given subject. These beliefs impact your viewpoint on a variety of subjects including finances, personal goals, or even spirituality among others.

If you are now wondering how you have validated your belief system, the answer is easy; through the continuous life experiences we each share.

Each of your life experiences serve to reinforce your established belief system. Challenging your long held thought patterns with new truths or ideas, will first allow you the freedom to begin to change your current beliefs. Secondly, it will allow you to experience complete change that will be manifested in your outward life by embracing a new inward belief system.

A Selah Moment

*"You must know <u>the</u> truth,
because believing a truth
can lead you astray."*

— *S. Yvon Harper*

The Empire State Building

Most of us are familiar with New York's famous Empire State Building. While I have never been to its top, it was impressed in my mind as a child when I saw the movie King Kong. Afterwards, I recall how my brothers and I pretended to build that famous building with our toy building blocks. We would agonize and strategize before precisely placing each colored block upon the other until our desired masterpiece was completed. As you might imagine, the final product was not a true representation of that great building. However, as children our accomplishment was worth more than how the building actually looked. We had achieved something "extraordinary" out of ordinary blocks, because we believed we would not fail.

Our expertise grew with every new project. Each presented new challenges for us to overcome. Sometimes we discovered that only wide blocks could be used. Other times we were unsure of how to proceed past a certain point. At any rate, the process was the same before beginning any new project. We always assessed the tools we had to work with, as well as, the skills required to successfully complete the project.

While our thoughts are not as tangible as our toy building blocks, consider them as internal building blocks positioned within your mind and just as real. Left unchecked they may allow you to approach new truths without a sound foundation to build upon. Take the following exercises, Building Blocks vs. Stumbling Blocks, designed to reveal what you may already know about your own internal strengths and weaknesses.

Building Blocks can be used to create new accomplishments, while Stumbling Blocks present themselves as obstacles to keep you from achieving your desired goals. The written answers you provide will serve as a reference point for you. First read each question, and then take time to Selah, meditate and reflect, before answering. These foundational questions will help you identify blocks and determine if they are Building Blocks, valuable for use reinforcing your strengths, growing your courage and building your self-confidence, or Stumbling Blocks which need to be earmarked for disposal that can keep your foundation in a constant state of repair costing you precious time.

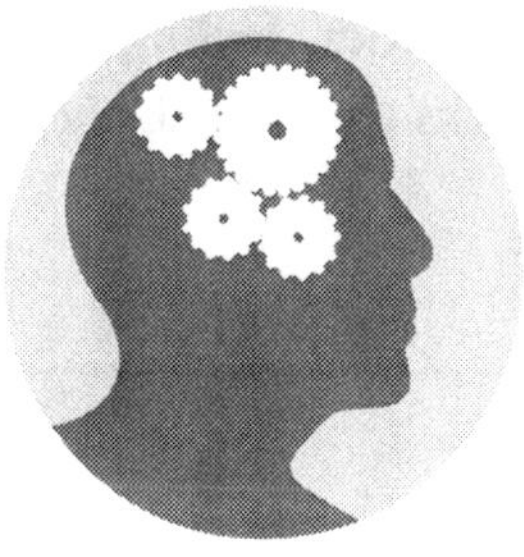

Discovery Exercise: Stumbling Blocks vs. Building Blocks

A Name your goal:

____

____

____

____

____

____

____

____

B In your own words describe those characteristics, feelings and thoughts you consider to be Stumbling Blocks that are obstacles to achieving your goal:

____

____

____

____

____

____

____

____

____

____

Describe a personal experience that highlights your example:

D Describe the qualities, strengths and talents you consider to be Building Blocks that are available to help achieve your goal:

____

____

____

____

____

____

____

____

____

____

____

E   Describe a personal experience that highlights your example:

____

____

____

____

____

____

____

____

____

____

____

Stumbling Blocks

Think about and identify the specific areas of your life in which you desire to see changes. Use the space provided below to list up to five beliefs (characteristics, traits, emotions, thoughts, etc.) that have served as Stumbling Blocks in your process to make changes.

1) ____

____

2) ____

____

3) ____

____

4) ____

____

5) ____

____

Building Blocks

Next, list five beliefs that you hold true and that you feel have the potential to immediately act as a foundation to erect Building Blocks for your process of making positive and productive life changes.

1 ____

____

2 ____

____

3 ____

____

4 ____

____

5 ____

____

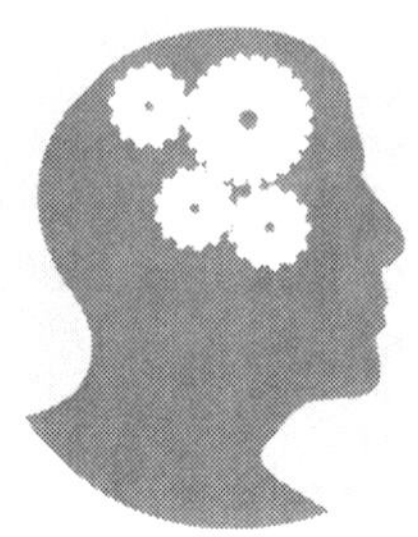

Discovery Question: Review

A Review your list of Blocks. Now, when approaching a new challenge, think about which Blocks you automatically reach for first? Explain why?

REDEFINE, REALIGN
AND
REDESIGN YOUR LIFE
FROM THE
INSIDE OUT

CHAPTER TWO

The Influence Pool

A Selah Moment

"Influence is a silent partner of decision making. It can lead you to victory or just as easily to defeat. You must first know from which direction the influence came."

— *S. Yvon Harper*

What Influences?

In the previous chapter you were asked to list your own personal beliefs regarding Stumbling Blocks that you may encounter in your journey to transformation. Equally as important, you listed the required Building Blocks necessary for a fresh transformation to occur. Now, let's examine how you know whether the things you listed will work in conjunction with your efforts to build a "new you".

Think about how you arrived at the point where you could clearly identify the steps you selected. Where did these steps come from? Are you the "owner" of these steps or are they a combination of the influence of others and your life experiences? Drilling down to answer these questions will bring greater clarity, allowing you to clearly find your way on this new and exciting journey.

Vegetable Delight

I remember around the age of six voicing the statement, "When I grow up I'm not going to eat vegetables!" This trailed after just being told, by my parents, that I would lose out on dessert, if I did not clean off my plate of vegetables. Regardless, even after my parent's best effort to persuade me, my feelings about vegetables were grounded in my self's foundation at the tender age of six!

It has been a battle, formed between me and the vegetables, for me to get past my prejudice regarding consuming vegetables. Only during the last few years have I taken the opportunity to revisit my stand to boycott all vegetables. However, this came about only after a lengthy conversation with my doctor on the importance of eating vegetables for weight control and their effectiveness in fighting off various diseases. My doctor's influence led me to reassess my decision.

Like many others, you may not have always agreed with certain views held by your family members, teachers or social leaders. However, in the formative years of your life, especially during adolescence, you may have found yourself making decisions based upon those earlier influences. Looking back it really doesn't matter whether the outcome of those decisions were good or bad. More importantly is the influence that these types of authority figures had and how their influence impacted your subconscious thoughts and resulting actions. It must also be recognized that influences come from not only interactions with people, but also from your growing experiences with places or things as well.

What Am I Thinking?

In order to establish permanent change in our thought process, one step we must take is identifying why we believe what we believe.

Our beliefs form the underlying foundation of every action we take. Each action is based on the fundamental thoughts of others who have influenced and had an impact on our own thought processes from other sources that have impacted us. For me the avoidance of vegetables in favor of other foods, which were heavy on sugar, can be traced back to my parent's rule of denying me dessert for not eating my vegetables. Unknowingly, I had been protesting their actions for a good portion of my adult life. If you had asked me "why don't you eat vegetables?" I simply would have answered "because I don't like them".

As I stated, it took knocking down this "stumbling block" to begin a new thought pattern about my belief that all vegetables were bad and acknowledge that my parents were actually right. In fact I can now honestly proclaim, my body needs vegetables and as a result I have enjoyed adding their variety to my menu. Not to mention, I have come to appreciate the 30 pounds of weight loss I achieved after ending my vegetable boycott!

To be clear, the idea here is not about eating vegetables. More so, it is to make a point that without the benefit of questioning yourself about why you embrace your current beliefs, you may never discover the unknown benefits of new choices.

It is important to understand that all actions are governed by an influence whether good or bad. By taking time to acknowledge that you have these influences and to learn to recognize which ones will assist you in knocking down those Stumbling Blocks is quite a breakthrough. You will discover that as you knock down these Stumbling Blocks, you start replacing them with Building Blocks and begin to realize the hidden influences that have such a profound affect on us. By choosing to follow all the positive influences within us, we begin to see a dramatic change and transformation allowing this positive influence to "speak" for us.

Influence Speaks

When you make a statement, it is a reflection of your thoughts and as a result we are come to be known by what we speak. For example: If, as a child, you were taught to fear black cats, because of superstitious beliefs from your grandmother, that influence may have caused you to grow up exhibiting that irrational fear, without a valid explanation. The caution for you and I is to again validate why we believe the thing that we believe.

We can often begin this process of validation by reconsidering some of our family's values and beliefs. For instance, many of us grew up with the notion that "money is the root of all evil". This may have caused you to grow up feeling that all rich people are evil. You may even have expressed these feeling in words and actions by avoiding the company of people with money.

In my own experience as a child I recall hearing this citation from the Bible quoted frequently. Usually it was in connection to a person's unfortunate financial situation. Money is evil was a belief in our economic-social community, which carried the implication that less was more or less was better. Imagine my surprise, years later, when I finally reconsidered my belief and actually evaluated it by reading the biblical passage for myself. It actually reads "the *love* of money is the root of all evil" with the emphasis not on money itself or the lack thereof, but on the harmful effects that an irrational love of money can produce.

As an adult responsible for your own finances, it is important to consider how this saying or others like it may be influencing your current financial choices and life decisions.

For me it was empowering to discover that less was not more and that having more was good, if kept in the proper perspective. Knowing and understanding this one truth will allow you to make wiser choices concerning your finances rather than solely being influenced by those beliefs of family, friends and others.

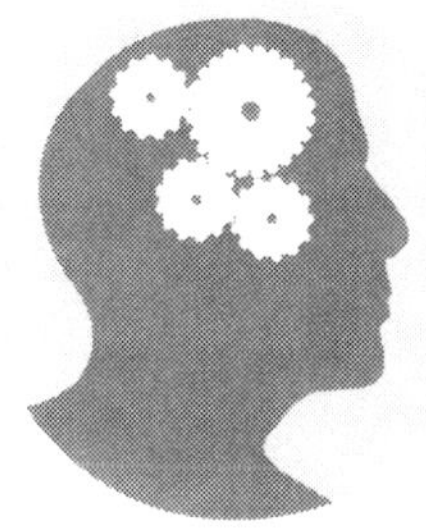

Discovery Exercise:
The Power of Influence

A Take a moment to examine the clichés, sayings, ideas or proverbs that you have repeatedly heard and accepted without validation.

A1 Which of them govern decisions in your life today?

____

____

____

____

____

____

____

A2 How have you been influenced by these types of statements?

____

____

____

____

____

____

____

____

____

____

____

____

B List at least two or more specific life influences, whether positive or negative, in the space provided below. Describe how they are making an impact on your life today. Ask yourself "why do I hold on to them?" Do not forget to note whether the influence stems from a person, place or thing.

List quotations from the past that still impact your life today. Example: "Romance without finance is a nuisance."

REDEFINE, REALIGN
AND
REDESIGN YOUR LIFE
FROM THE
INSIDE OUT

CHAPTER THREE

Choosing a New Path

A Selah Moment

"Most travelers have found that getting to a desired path is seldom as hard as staying on it once you begin the journey."

— *S. Yvon Harper*

Now What?

Up to this point we have been evaluating and challenging your thoughts, feelings and actions against old influences, processes and beliefs. By showing you how to choose those powerful, positive influences, you have learned how to knock down those "stumbling blocks" that at one point looked insurmountable, threatening and way too difficult to even move. You now find yourself creating, positive and permanent changes that will allow you to prosper, but the process doesn't stop here. This process is ever-growing and never stops progressing. You must continue to review, meditate and question your thoughts daily. By allowing any negative thinking into even the tiniest area of your mind, you risk contaminating all the positive elements you have worked so hard to achieve! So, with that in mind, we can move forward to the next step by continuing to choose exploring a new path and looking for ways to improve our mindset.

Let's begin by examining the 10 Steps of "W.A.I.T!" that will guide you on a journey towards permanent change. As with every journey one takes, this requires preparation. This journcy is different; this journey is your very own personal journey that will be filled with bumps, ups and downs, fast curves, and sometimes even traffic jams. Along the way you will encounter people, places and things that may join you on your journey to change; but then there may be those who will attempt to discourage you because like many, they "fear" change.

As you advance with each new step, you may find that your tolerance level for those friends and acquaintances that remain unchanged will begin to decrease. As you have committed to making this journey, you will find that it has an impact on those who are a part of your current inner circle. In fact, you may unknowingly become a mirror in which they examine themselves. Unfortunately what they see may not always be positive as they compare themselves to the positive strides that you are taking.

Crossroads

This is where you can find yourself at a crossroad, asking yourself whether to go on with your change process or whether to go back to that old comfortable feeling that leads to nowhere. Each time you encounter an obstacle, remember to hold on to the new knowledge you have received up to this point. You will need this new found knowledge to continue along your journey to grow and remain committed towards your transformation.

"W.A.I.T!" is a powerful source of real truth regarding personal change. The 10 Steps found in this book are richly powerful! They will impact your life, if you are willing to apply them in your everyday life.

In the next segment, we will look at the 10 Steps you must take to effectively change your life permanently. Each step is specifically staged to equip, empower and motivate you to *Redefine, Realign and Redesign Your Life from the Inside Out*. Be alert, as you will discover each of the 10 Steps is designated by a powerful heading which will assist you in identifying your progress.

Are you ready for the positive, permanent change that will take place in your life? I'm sure your answer is a confident "yes". You have already begun this journey by selecting this book. So let's proceed!

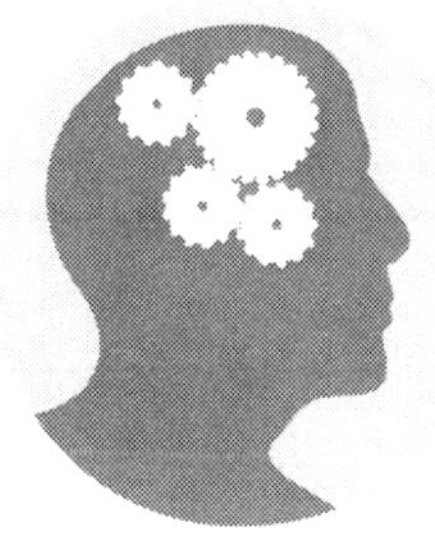

Discovery Exercise: Permanent Change

A Describe the areas you have chosen to create a permanent change in your life.

B List the people in your inner circle.

How might they support your changes in this journey?

D What new knowledge can you hold onto when you encounter challenges, obstacles or discouragement?

REDEFINE, REALIGN
AND
REDESIGN YOUR LIFE
FROM THE
INSIDE OUT

STEP ONE

Self Realization of Honesty

A Selah Moment

*"To discover a jewel is divine,
but to discover it within
oneself is precious."*

— S. Yvon Harper

Start With Honesty

Identifying what you are thinking in the area you are targeting for change requires total honesty and a deep exploration of your current thoughts. Honesty is a key component in your journey toward permanent change. The unfortunate impact of discovering dishonesty can be life altering.

I have seen several cases of this within my Focus on Finance clientele. As you continue to progress through the 10 Steps I will share various scenarios with you in order to provide examples of key concepts. One example I will refer to is a case couple whom we shall call Sean and Donna Rich to protect their identities.

The Rich's had made several attempts on their own to maximize their finances without achieving the desired level of success before seeking professional counsel. During one session with Sean and Donna I asked them to complete a cash flow tracking exercise for review at their next visit. Sean was comfortable with the request, however, Donna was reluctant. Several attempts were made to address her uneasiness, but in the end the activity was postponed for a later date.

About a week later, I received a surprising call from Donna, who confided that her reason for concern was not the exercise itself, but what it would reveal. She went on to reveal that her portrayal of her spending habits to Sean had not been honest. Such as purchases Donna had made and then hid from Sean. The fear of facing this dishonesty with her husband and the reaction he might have had paralyzed her with fear and kept her from moving forward with the exercise.

The emphasis placed on honesty is never exaggerated. If you have lived your life being dishonest and have never faced this giant, before you continue with your journey, now would be the time to come face to face and confront this realization. First with yourself and then with others that may have been affected. You'll find that the momentary discomfort of doing so will not compare with the newfound freedom awaiting you. It is a huge step for someone not accustomed to honesty, to make such a complete turnaround and admit being dishonest just doesn't work.

Two Keys: Wisdom and Discernment

In being honest you will need to utilize two key attributes, namely wisdom and discernment. Without these attributes, you will not be fully able to implement their applications in correcting dishonest or misleading past mistakes. Otherwise you risk putting at stake the loss of your creditability and respectability.

Honesty means being open without deception. Discernment means balancing wisdom with honesty. This is key as you will learn that discernment helps you to recognize who and when, while wisdom dictates how much to share, and you will need to master both. Wisdom and discernment are strong helpmates that will accompany you on your journey.

Don't be confused, this does not mean that you need to become a master at deliberately withholding the truth. That is deception. Instead, you will discover that some of your past experiences are not physically or emotionally feasible to revisit directly, because of the toll they have already taken on the parties involved. In these circumstances your wisdom and discernment should lead to repentance for the indiscretions committed without those parties direct involvement. Now you can move forward by not repeating the same mistake again.

On the next page list as much as possible about your beliefs concerning your target thought area. Include in your list the source of your beliefs or thoughts. This may include specific incidents that have impacted your target area. In particular, put into practice being honest with you first. Be aware that you will only delay your own progress towards any productive change you are working towards, if you are not completely honest.

Self realization and complete honesty leads to becoming a person of integrity and principles. Listing your beliefs regarding your target area is crucial, so proceed with the exercise and discover your possibilities.

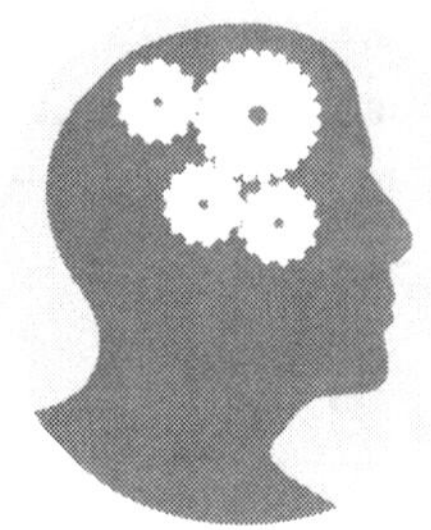

Discovery Exercise:
Step One – Defining
Your Target

A Describe in detail your target area. Reference the paragraph chapter one for assistance:

____

____

____

____

____

____

____

____

____

B Identify any associated negative thoughts:

Explain how these thoughts became a part of your belief? Where did they originate?

D What people or things have influenced your target thoughts?

REDEFINE, REALIGN
AND
REDESIGN YOUR LIFE
FROM THE
INSIDE OUT

STEP TWO

Making a Quality Decision

A Selah Moment

"The ability to stand firm in the affirmation of your own values when others oppose them is a character quality of great worth."

— *S. Yvon Harper*

Decisions, Decisions

Once you have honestly identified the negative and unproductive thoughts associated with your target area, you must begin to make quality decisions in order to take action with those thoughts and behaviors. To go through the identification process without addressing the underlying issue is useless. It would be like having the answer to a million dollar question, but refusing to hit the bell to respond. That's nonsense!

Recall Donna's story about her habit of overspending. If she had chosen to reveal this truth, but then decided not to address it, she would have continued to live with her "giant". Fortunately, Donna was willing to take the next step by making a quality decision to do something about it. In Step Two you are now being required to address your personal target area.

The decisions you make during this step in the process, form the foundation for your success. In many instances, I have observed individuals who waiver at this step. Though they desire the freedom that is before them, they feel unable to let go of past behaviors. If you find yourself in this position, then "W.A.I.T!" Literally pause and ask yourself, *"What am I thinking?"* and why am I thinking this? Your honest answers will clearly reveal the source of the obstacles that hinder your progress.

Most often, the number one obstacle many of us fear is fear itself. Fear of success, fear of failure, and most of all, fear of the unknown. Our fears serve as a powerful opponent. However, knowing the truth will set you free from the grip of fear. Remember the following definition of what fear actually is each time it attempts to take hold of you.

It is nothing more than:

Fear is an illusion of what *could* be. It is not the realization of what *is*. Decision making can be a tedious process. It is not always as straightforward as it appears on the surface. Nonetheless, most of the important decisions in our lives will require that we drill down past our comfort zones. Moving past this point is not easy. It is downright difficult in most instances. You have become familiar and comfortable with your current choices, but in order to progress, you must "sweep" out the attic!

Rest assured that with determination and God's help, it can be done. The decision to move to the next level comes with a price. The price is commitment, faith, courage and belief in your own God given abilities. Not only the abilities you currently boast, but those that you will develop with each step in the "W.A.I.T!" process.

As you start the development process of growing these important attributes, you will become aware of the extreme importance and meaning of "choice". Do not be deceived, the choice is solely yours to make. Once, I had an encounter with a prospective client who was armed with a list of challenges they believed kept them from financial freedom from debt. Though solutions were suggested to their challenges, the client continued to come up with new roadblocks to moving forward. Most of their reservations were related to what others perceived regarding their situation. This client chose to allow these perceptions to influence their thinking. The fear of rising above this influence consequently prevented them from making the quality decisions they needed in order to progress and attain their desired goal. Don't let this happen to you. Make the decision to proceed and don't waiver from it.

In the space provided, in your own words, write a *Personal Decision Declaration Statement* regarding the "target" area you have identified in Step One. This statement should include your intentions to diligently identify, address and discard any thought that does not line up with the new direction you have chosen to undertake in your life. It may reference quotes, pictures, music and other symbols that will describe the permanent change you are to create. Be sure to be as detailed as possible and if necessary, use additional pieces of paper to complete. Post this statement in a prominent place, then review it daily!

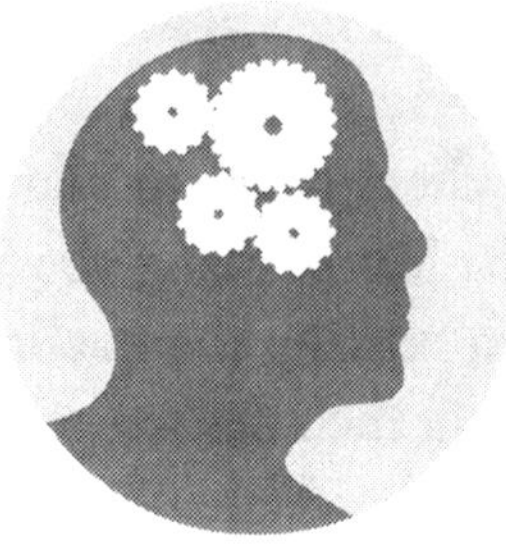

***Discovery Exercise:
Step Two – Creating a
Personal Declaration***

Write a Personal Decision Declaration Statement regarding the target area you have honestly identified to address in Step One. You may reference quotes, pictures, music and other symbols that will describe the permanent change you are to create. Print and post your declaration in a place where you can review it frequently.

Redefine, Realign
And
Redesign your life
From The
INSIDE OUT

STEP THREE

Renew Your Mind

A Selah Moment

"Take heed, for as a person thinks in his heart, his feet will soon follow."

— S. Yvon Harper

Eliminating Sacred Cows

As you approach this third step, you should be secure in your new decision to address your targeted area of change. Next, you must begin discarding everything that does not line up with the new truths you are choosing to accept. Let me be clear that I do mean *everything*. This means that you must not only discard your old thoughts, but also begin the process of replacing them with new, positive thoughts. A sacred cow is described by the Wikipedia Encyclopedia as "something which cannot be tampered with, or criticized, for fear of public outcry". For total success to take place there can be no sacred cows left behind, because they will become hindrances in your journey.

To do this, you must seek new resources and establish a foundation of wisdom, which means accumulated knowledge or enlightenment. In my own journey, I used a combination, because one source did not fit every challenge. The sources included people whom I admire who are positive, honest and live with ethics having a sense of moral and godly responsibility, because they represented my new direction. Your direction and resources could be in the form of personal conversations, an article, or a book you read that addresses the needs to strengthen the areas of your present weakness. Even visiting new places can be a resource for support.

Self Talk

Another excellent tool to begin utilizing is *self-talk*. This is the ability to directly impact your beliefs by replacing negative thoughts with positive thoughts by speaking the positive thoughts to yourself. This type of communication straightforwardly supports your efforts to renew your mind. Don't worry, that people will think you are a little odd for talking to yourself out loud, in most cases your speech is done internally. *Renewal Statements* are another component of implementing self talk. Instead of verbal modification they are written statements used to serve as a visual change agent of new positive thoughts.

For example, if your target is dealing with self-esteem and the associated negative thought is "I'm never going to succeed" you would begin to use self talk to replace the negative statement with positive statements such as "Nothing is going to stop me this time!" A written renewal statement using these declarations help keep you focused on your new path.

It is a little known fact that when comparing what other people say with our internal self talk on the same subject, that the impact of an individual's self talk is more powerful than any positive statement from outside sources. That is because, subconsciously, we are wired to believe what we say to ourselves more than what anyone else says to us. An example of this is when a person is offered a compliment, but is unwilling to accept it as truth. Until the receiver of the compliment is willing to accept or believe the positive feedback, the message will have very little impact. In other words they have a need to speak positively to themselves. The results from *self-talk* and *renewal statements* will astound you and serve as a powerful reinforcement of your new way of thinking.

Self Reflection

If you are approaching this step with another person each of you will need to complete this step independently. You may come across similar ideas or thoughts, but the degree to which they influence your decisions may vary. This was true with our study case of the Rich's.

When Sean and Donna Rich first approached this step, it was important to isolate their separate negative influences. They had been married for several years and each felt very in tune with the other's thought patterns. Even so, the influences to their target area, as you will see were different.

During this step they discovered a common target thought, which was "I will never be free from debt." However, the influence of this belief for Sean stemmed from his continued investment in unworthy financial shortcuts. On the other hand, for Donna this belief fueled her habit to overspend. Both were required to independently address the behaviors associated with this common thought separately.

There is a compelling proverb in the Bible that says, "As a man thinks in his heart so is he". Each of us is more aware of our innermost thoughts, fears and dreams than anyone else. Assuredly, I can attest to this fact. After nineteen years of marriage my husband still manages to surprise me, but I in turn continue to surprise him by my thoughts as well. Conclusion…do not underestimate the importance of this step.

Consider what thoughts you have this very moment regarding the influences that you have begun to confront. What have you negatively told yourself about your target area up to this point? Keep that in mind as you proceed to the Discovery Questions on the next page.

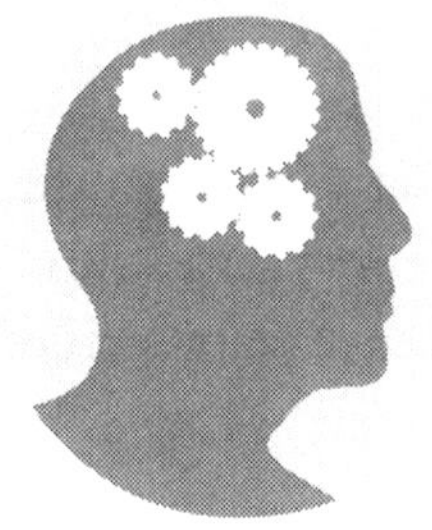

Discovery Exercise: Step Three – Renewal Statements

Renewal Statements serve as change agents in the battle to impact negative thought behavior. Below create a resource list of personal statements to provide you with encouragement. Place them in a location where you will be able to read or record them to replay daily. Note: As you go along, many of your statements will continue to evolve to impact various new target areas.

REDEFINE, REALIGN
AND
REDESIGN YOUR LIFE
FROM THE
INSIDE OUT

STEP FOUR

Boundaries

A Selah Moment

*"The placement of any fence always
serves the greater purpose to save
from harm what one purposes
to preserve within its walls."*

— S. Yvon Harper

Setting Boundaries

Why must you establish boundaries? Remember the old saying: "If you continue to do what you've always done; you will continue to get what you've always gotten". We are declaring that we want something new and there is no place for old negative thoughts, habits, patterns, or people.

It will be necessary for you to establish for yourself and others, limits of what will be allowed in your backyard as you journey towards change. Basically, this means you must identify what the boundaries are concerning your "target" area. Boundaries can be described as limits or borders. Think of a sign that warns others to keep out and signals you to stay away.

For example, when establishing boundaries in the area of personal finance those boundaries might include spending limits. Imagine that a person desires to establish new spending habits and to get out of debt. It is obvious that if they continue to overspend, they will not accomplish their new goal. A new boundary they might establish could be deciding not to carry credit cards or checkbooks. Another boundary they could create would be to completely avoid going to the store if it is not within the means of their budget. Even if they see items or products being advertised as the greatest sale of the year!

Boundaries will help to ensure your success by minimizing exposure to things that would take you off track. It is essential to avoid compromise once you have established your boundaries.

Case in Point

Recall Sean and Donna in our case study. Sean had a passion for browsing the weekly sale ads for the latest electronic gadgets on the market. He already had a small arsenal of phones, audio devices, and personal computer paraphernalia. Donna and he both admitted that these unplanned expenditures had caused havoc on their budget. Sean defended these past purchases as necessary to effectively track his financial investments. However, after the Rich's identified the need to establish a sound budget, before pursuing additional investments, the newest electronic gadgets were no longer Sean's top priority.

Realizing his weakness, Sean set limitations and requested Donna's help in establishing new spending boundaries. He no longer allowed himself to browse the weekly sale ads. As his back-up Donna became what I refer to as his accountability partner, challenging Sean's many impulse purchases. Sean not only began to tell himself that he didn't need new equipment, but looked for opportunities to cash in on the excessive electronic devices he currently owned. The Rich's also started planning for these types of expenditures in their newly formed budget.

Was this an easy transition for Sean? Perhaps not, but the rewards of diligently establishing boundaries for protection of his budget was a quality decision. The benefits Sean and Donna have experienced include: elimination of disagreements about over-spending, better control of their monetary funds and a savings plan that will allow them to make contributions in the investment market sooner than expected.

Instituting your personal boundaries will also produce positive outcomes that support your new goals. The key to success in setting boundaries lies in making them measurable, obtainable and realistic.

For Sean and Donna this meant creating a sound budget including establishing a "rainy" day fund for future emergencies. You may even find it necessary to request help, which we will talk more about in an upcoming step. Likewise, failure to achieve your goals can be directly tied to the failure to set appropriate boundaries.

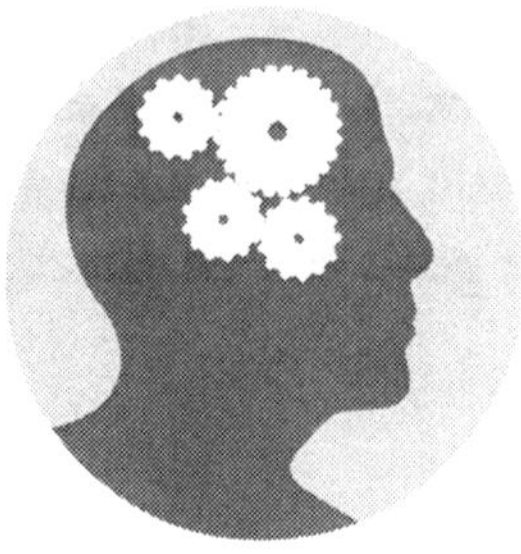

Discovery Exercise:
Step Four – Boundaries

A For each example below list possible boundaries for the target area identified such as:

A1 I want to lose weight.

A2 I want to quit gossiping.

A3 I want to stop being so negative with my words.

B List below the boundaries you are setting for your personal target area. I want to:

Redefine, Realign
And
Redesign your life
From The
inside out

STEP FIVE

Protection From Over Exposure

A Selah Moment

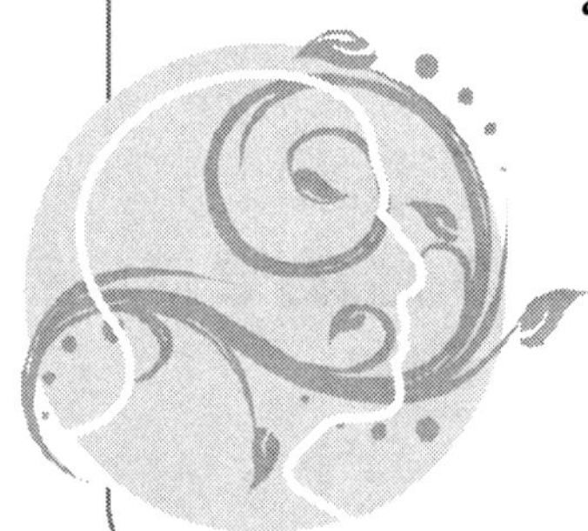

"Wisdom always stands as the gatekeeper against folly."

— S. Yvon Harper

Fences

So far, you have been honest with yourself in identifying and acknowledging target areas, making decisions to address them, taking steps to replace unproductive thoughts with positive ones and setting boundaries. Next, you must put up your "fence" for protection. What does this mean and how is it different from boundaries? It means that you must begin to protect yourself from negative over exposure from any source not aligned with your new path. This can only be done by correctly selecting and establishing what you will do, whom you will do it with, and where you will allow yourself to go, thus putting up a fence. This vital step serves to protect you from unnecessary negativity concerning the target areas you are choosing to address.

Although this may seem similar to establishing boundaries, it is a uniquely different step. In the last step you established *who* and *what* you would allow into your backyard. Now you must put in place the "fence" not only to keep out trespassers, but also to restrict your voluntary access to them. For example, you will need to limit exposure to anything that does not support your new goals. If you are to break free from old addictions you cannot permit yourself to visit former places where people are involved with that type of addiction. Nor can those people, places or things be allowed beyond the protection of your 'fence' to visit you.

It was a sobering day for Donna Rich when she made the choice to decline shopping luncheons with her friends, Sara and Tammy. Until this point Donna had felt comfortable indulging her spending indiscretions with her friends. What changed? Donna's new found commitment to begin living within her new spending plan. The temptation Sara and Tammy presented for Donna to step outside the protection of her "fence" no longer held the same enticement that reaching her newly established goal now held.

Selective Solitude

Recall that as we started this section I explained that everyone is not going to support you in your efforts to move towards positive change. Some will be pessimists. Others will continue with their own unconstructive behavior in your presence. While you do not have control of what others do, you do have control of what they do around you. Therefore, you must reconsider everything you had been accustomed to doing, activities you usually engaged in, places you enjoyed going and even people you enjoyed being with that would impede your progress.

This step is not always easy, but rest assured as you continue the practice of protecting yourself from over exposure to unproductive actions and situations, people will notice your new commitment to change. Some may even stop associating with you as a result, but others who support or share in your new mindset will soon replace them. At this step, it is vital that no matter what you DON'T COMPROMISE on your new beliefs!

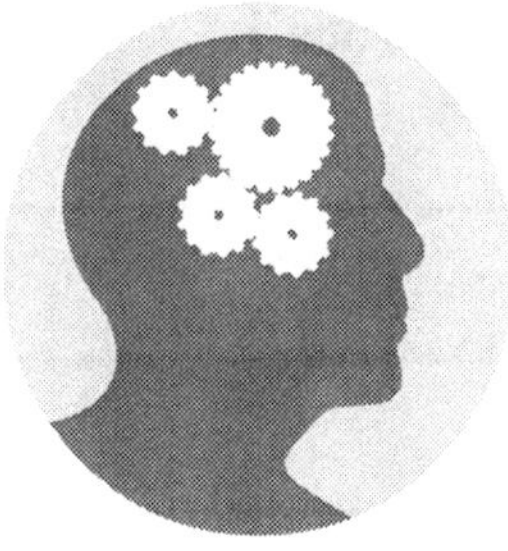

Discovery Exercise:
Step Five – Protection from Overexposure

A List the places, activities or events that you attend or engage in that might compromise your new commitment and goals.

____

____

____

____

____

____

____

____

B   In what areas or situations will you require a "fence"?

C. List the actions you will take to protect yourself from overexposure. Be specific.

____

____

____

____

____

____

____

____

____

____

____

REDEFINE, REALIGN
AND
REDESIGN YOUR LIFE
FROM THE
INSIDE OUT

STEP SIX

Say Goodbye
to the Past

A Selah Moment

"The indiscretions from my past have little effect on my life today. Not just because I've been forgiven, but because I have also chosen to forgive myself."

— S. Yvon Harper

Change

The American Heritage Dictionary describes *change* as *"to lay aside, abandon, or leave for another"*. On your new journey towards change you will find that you must disassociate yourself not only from places, people and things, but also from your past in order to continue moving forward. The past you want to leave behind includes the heavy load of failure, guilt, hurt, disappointments, condemnations and sadness. During this step, it is important that you lighten your load by leaving it behind and by stepping into the "now" without all that extra weight of your past.

Changing or controlling the past while living in the "now" is like the hamster that keeps going around on the wheel and going nowhere. Chances are that you know people who struggle with their "present" because they choose to dwell in the "past", so all their "present" actions are really based on their past life experiences.

Disassociation with your past will ensure that you will not walk the path back to your unproductive life style. Instead keep your commitment to keep transforming in the present so that your future will lead you into a life filled with positive, productive and inspiring actions.

It is likely that you will find yourself being challenged as was the case with the Rich's. They found themselves struggling to overcome the past fears and mistrust they had created when they were busy blaming one another for their financial circumstances. Fortunately, their mutual desire to fulfill the promise of successful future accomplishments gave them the strength they needed to overcome those issues, which were once obstacles. Together they were able to walk through the dark shadows that had consumed them during those rough times.

Forgiveness

One of the most important characteristics to possess and demonstrate is one that can often be difficult to show, especially in the world we live in where it is often mistaken as a sign of weakness. Because of this tendency to view it as a weakness, people often choose not to display it for fear of being seen as weak. But contrary to that misconception, it is in fact a show of great strength and requires another powerful characteristic known as humility.

During your process of change, it is a crucial step to learn how to demonstrate forgiveness in order to accelerate your transformation. When you are able to forgive, it leads to a new level of freedom. By taking the focus off yourself and placing it on another, you also become unselfish. All these characteristics serve to free you from the negative, even dangerous feelings of anger, rebellion, frustration, and seeking revenge, which can often lead to ulcers, stomach problems and even heart attacks.

The act of forgiveness is wholly unselfish. It requires that you take the focus away from yourself by placing it on another. This is because the act of forgiveness is the relinquishing of your sole right to exercise your right. It says "I release you from the bondage of restitution, my anger, disappointment, and the need to apologize". Those receiving the pardon of forgiveness seldom understand the giver of such pardon is truly receiving the greatest benefit from this gracious act.

Personally, I can recall how the act of forgiveness spearheaded some major successes in my own life. I had developed feelings of disappointment towards certain individuals that had caused me to move toward bitterness for personal reasons. It was not until I forgave these individuals that I was able to move ahead towards my own aspirations. Amazingly, the process of forgiveness took place in my heart without the individuals ever knowing what had happened. Still, that action of forgiveness provided me the freedom to overcome those obstacles that had blocked me from reaching my goals. One of which is this book which you are now reading.

Harboring unforgiveness hinders your ability to recognize new opportunities that stand before you. Unforgiveness takes precious time and energy. Keeps you focused on the negative rather than all the positive energy that can exist in your life. I've had clients who would not resolve past differences with a spouse, family member or friend. Each attempt to introduce new financial possibilities to them was overshadowed by the negative emotions they harbored towards these individuals. The result was missed opportunities and unfulfilled ambitions for these clients. In most cases, the individuals that these clients targeted had moved on towards their own goals.

In closing, the last point I want to make is that this process is *"all about you"*. Learning forgiveness is a major part of your transformation. By not learning to forgive, you will impede your progress.

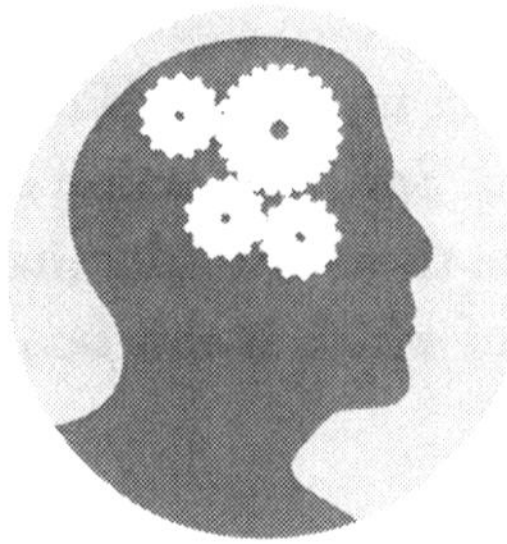

Discovery Exercise:
Step Six – Forgiveness

A Reflect on any incident where unforgiveness has been given space to dwell in the past. Briefly list the event(s) below:

____

____

____

____

____

____

____

____

____

____

B Why do you devote time to dwell on it?

C. What feeling is associated with this past event and or person (fear, anger, hurt)?

D How has this past event or person affected your life in the present?

Make a decision today to forgive everyone in your life, as necessary, and free yourself from the burden of unforgiveness. You will receive the ultimate benefit from being free.

REDEFINE, REALIGN
AND
REDESIGN YOUR LIFE
FROM THE
INSIDE OUT

Correction and Direction

A Selah Moment

"Correction provides direction…so always be ready to change your course."

— S. Yvon Harper

Wisdom's Benefits

It happens to be the greatest book in the world. One of the bestselling books, the oldest book and the wisest book. Yes, I am talking about the book of the Bible. It is filled with information regarding the benefits of wisdom or the lack thereof. Throughout the book of Proverbs it speaks about accepting correction and taking direction. How does this relate to establishing permanent change? Recall in Step Six where we identified change as "to lay aside, abandon, or leave for another". One way this is done is through the correction of our current ways and the acceptance of a new direction.

Essentially, it is divine wisdom that allows us to accept correction and receive direction, because we each are in control of our own free will. Especially when the wisdom offered is not catered to our individual preferences or tastes. Personally, I would prefer to pay attention to someone else's mistakes rather than making the same ones and suffering the consequences myself. However, when I was younger I did not value this concept. Consequently, I suffered needlessly. Thank God that I finally found and cultivated wisdom!

In practical terms imagine that you were traveling down a road at a high rate of speed. An oncoming car flashed their lights to give you a warning to slow down. Wouldn't you be glad that they did before a law officer around the corner, with ticket in hand, discovered you speeding? I know that I would have been happy to receive this opportunity to self correct my speed based on their direction. You may think this is a simple example, but I can tell you that I have seen people disregard these types of warning to their own expense.

The Cost of Rejecting Wisdom

People often reject wisdom when it is offered. Accepting correction and receiving direction requires humility. Because some have been fooled into believing "I'm in control" or that "It's my choice" not to partake of the wisdom offered to them.

This is especially true if what is being offered does not line up with your own belief. This mindset has caused many to keep traveling with blinders on down the same road towards destruction. Several years ago I heard the need for this type of wisdom best stated as "Correction provides direction". It is needless for you to suffer numerous mistakes when wisdom provided by others can assist you in avoiding them. Insanity is defined as "doing the same thing over and over again, expecting different results." And as you know, this does not work.

You must not only ask yourself where you are headed on your journey for change, but also what roadmap you will use to get you there. Many are available to choose from, but if you accept correction by wisdom you will also receive direction that will lead you to greater success.

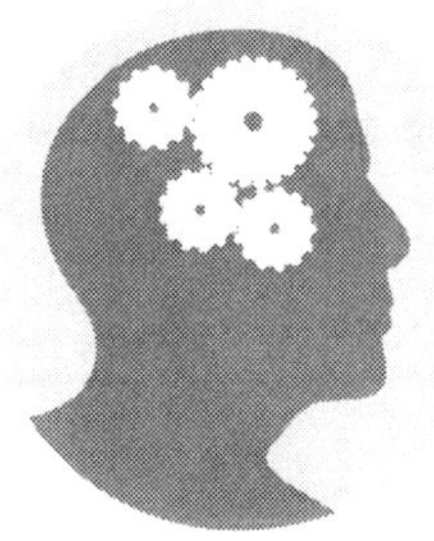

Discovery Exercise: Step Seven – Correction and Direction

A Think about your targeted area for permanent change. List the corrective guidance you have received regarding your goal.

B How has accepting correction impacted the course of your direction in the target area in which you are seeking a desired change?

REDEFINE, REALIGN
AND
REDESIGN YOUR LIFE
FROM THE
INSIDE OUT

Establishing a Support System

A Selah Moment

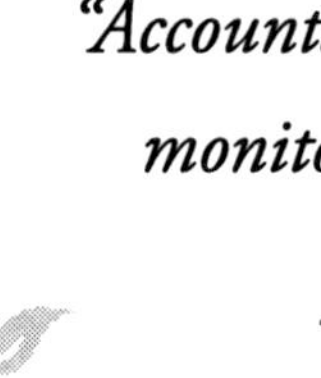

"Accountability is the hall monitor to success."

— S. Yvon Harper

The Accountability Factor

Accountability in its simplest form is the *action of being responsible to someone for some activity.* Basically, it is the idea that you will need to give up your right to be right. In order to answer to another person, other than yourself, for what you do or don't do.

A mandatory requirement for Step Eight is that you take great care in establishing and planning an accountability support system in order to remain successful. To be effective these partners must be committed and strong in their own walk. Notice I did not say they had to be perfect. The key is to look for individuals who are diligently walking in the "direction" you desire to go. It was John Donne who wrote the famous quote "No man is an island unto himself". This statement represents the fact that human beings need one another in order to help us survive.

In your own personal journey towards permanent change, you will discover this to be very true. By surrounding yourself with committed, positive and energetic people who share the same path as you, you establish a very important characteristic…accountability. This is your responsibility to ensure that if you stumble, or if you fall, there will be someone there to pick you up.

In the Bible's book of Galatians we are advised to help carry one another's burden and encouraged to walk with others who are putting forth an effort to move ahead. Following this advice helps in two important ways. First, it strengthens those who are challenged in moving into new, unknown areas, and secondly, it provides accountability to ensure that one's actions are correctly aligned with their stated path.

Support Your Vision

There may be times when individuals offer you support verbally, but offer no support in their actions. For example, someone may tell you, don't hesitate to call if you need something, but avoid you not knowing how to respond when you do call. These types of people offer no true support, so avoid them as a support partner. Instead, watch and observe those interactions with others to identify those on whom you can truly count on to provide accountability support. As you start identifying those who are unreliable, use your boundaries and limits to choose and separate those who you wish to accompany you.

Relevance Factor

Conversely, let me caution you ahead of time that as you select your accountability support partners it will be important to consider the *Relevance Factor*. This factor speaks specifically to the appointed time a designated support will be available to provide specific support for you. It does not mean that you will predetermine this period of time in advance. Just keep in mind that it is automatically appointed based on the goals you are seeking to accomplish.

You will recognize that a support's time is coming to an end when it no longer effectively supports you. The *Relevance Factor* then begins to confirm that it is time to redefine, realign and redesign your accountability support system for continued growth towards your ultimate goal. This may mean that an accountability partner's role may shift by increasing, decreasing or eliminating responsibility altogether based on progress against your stated goal. Appropriate new accountability partners and support should be selected as a result of your *Relevance Factor* changes.

Understanding that the *Relevance Factor* is a normal process in your journey will eliminate unnecessary discomfort when it is time for your accountability supports to transition into a new role.

Character Counts

Recently I began the process of establishing a mentor relationship with a well known community leader. I had observed this person for some time watching and examining whether or not their actions were of good character. When I approached her regarding being my mentor, I already knew the level of accountability I would need to establish. I needed her to know that I could be held accountable not only for my commitment, but for my actions in this mentoring relationship.

It is important that you keep in mind not only the people that you surround yourself with, but also places as well. This is because the places we frequent can often become obstacles on our road towards success. Suppose you are attending school that requires much studying on your part as a requirement. Establishing the library as a place that supports your efforts towards studying will produce better results than if you were to establish studying at a "chatty" friend's house; where you could expect to be constantly interrupted. Another example is if you have a tendency to overspend and blow your budget when you and your friend decide to meet at the mall for lunch. After lunch you walk around and find yourself shopping and spending money you shouldn't on purchases you don't really need. A much better choice would be to meet at the park and "brown bag" it, as an alternative, thereby saving yourself from overspending and at the same time giving support to your goal of achieving financial success.

You need to have a thorough understanding and knowledge of whatever support systems you put in place and how it will impact you either positively or negatively in your commitment to change. Hold yourself accountable for all of your choices. Whether it is the friends you surround yourself with, the places you find yourself in or the overall decisions you make. Be honest with yourself, evaluate your answers and make the necessary adjustments to conform to your new way of being to help keep you pointed in the right direction. Making better choices *now* sets you up with the habit of making better choices for the *future*.

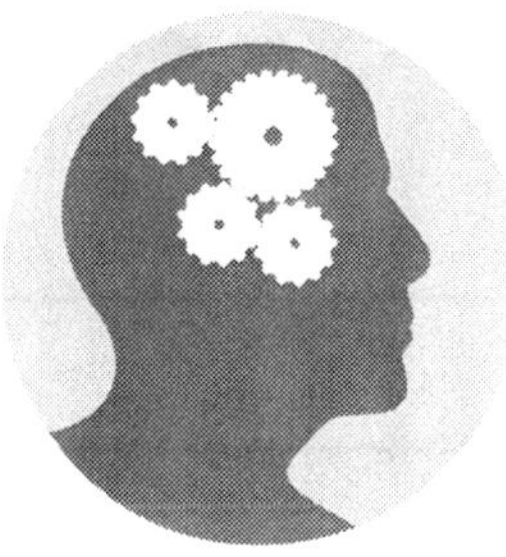

Discovery Exercise: Step Eight – Establishing a Support System

A What is the one accountability factor that must be in place for your success to materialize?

B Who will act as your accountability partner(s)? Why will he or she be effective in this role?

List the necessary characteristics for your accountability partner to have in place in order to be effective? Support them with your goals.

____

____

____

____

____

____

____

____

____

____

D List the goals that your accountability partner will hold you accountable for?

E Define when and how you will know that your accountability partner's role is no longer necessary or productive for you to continue achieving your stated goals?

REDEFINE, REALIGN
AND
REDESIGN YOUR LIFE
FROM THE
INSIDE OUT

STEP NINE

Walk It Out

A Selah Moment

"The journey of a thousand miles does not begin with the first step, but with the first thought."

— *S. Yvon Harper*

Planner vs. Doer Syndrome

We are probably acquainted with a person who is full of vibrant ideas. They are the ones who meticulously plan for every aspect of a new project. Any inquiry about execution is met with charts, graphs or even a dissertation of how the plan will be carried out. Then what happens? Time slips by without the enactment of any measurable progress towards the goal at hand. You sadly discover that you have met an individual infected with planner's syndrome.

It is hard to answer why some people never get past the planning stage. It ranks as one of the rhetorical wonders of life. It is impossible to identify who will get the syndrome and who will not. So the warning for you and I is to be on guard to take the next step at all costs. I'm not saying planning is not important, but that every feature of the plan need not be meticulously crafted, before it is enacted. You will have time to adjust the plan as necessary later.

You may recall our earlier discussion surrounding *fear*. In this step, to walk out and achieve your new goals, fear will take the opportunity to present itself as an obstacle. Believe me, as I speak from experience.

The Journey

Several years ago I was personally challenged with taking "W.A.I.T!" from my internal knowledge bank and creating the book you are now reading. Surprisingly, the challenge wasn't in creating the outline, but in facing the fear of successfully completing the task. I became infected with planner's syndrome for creating all the supporting strategies, but failed to execute completing the book. It was not until I took a large dose of my own medicine; following the steps outlined below that measurable progress was made. Notice that I was the only one who could initiate each of these nine steps:

Step One.............. I took a moment for self-reflection, which revealed that fear was present.

Step Two.............. I made a decision to write, no matter what, everyday.

Step Three........... I took a thorough examination of my internal barriers. I began to tell myself "I will complete this project".

Step Four............. I put boundaries in place to eliminate conflicting time distractions.

Step Five.............. I began to surround myself with people of like mindedness whose goals were productivity driven. Not just "well wishers".

Step Six............... I forgave myself for lost time in completing progress on the book.

Step Seven............ I listened to and applied instruction from successful authors on writing the book to avoid pitfalls.

Step Eight........... I engaged mentors who helped me become steady and focused to sort through and stick to my goals.

Step Nine............ I continued to walk out my outlined plans to make progress towards my goal of completing the "W.A.I.T!" book.

These steps were enacted even when I was fearful of the outcome, weary of the process and could not think of another word to write.

The result speaks for itself for you are now reading Step Nine of the finished goal. My reason for sharing my personal journey is that you might be encouraged to continue your own journey. Regardless of your current circumstances each of us has a need to target some area of our lives for improvement. Whether it is openly acknowledged or not, don't just plan to change, be in action by just doing it.

The Secret Key

A key factor in all of this is to have faith in your pending success. Let your abundance come from all the positive things you are taking on, not from monetary riches that does not guarantee a fulfilled and happy life. Let faith, hope and a new sense of integrity be your new companions in your life on the road towards success.

Hope and faith go hand in hand by strengthening your new bound belief system. Hope keeps you going when faith fails and you want to give up. There will be times when you may let your guard down and grow weary in the process. But continue to believe in yourself, continue to be true to yourself, continue to grow in all your positive attributes and characteristics that you have learned about and have started to apply in your life.

Don't compromise your principles or morals and by not doing so, you will continue to learn and live and accept the goodness and positivity that comes from living a life of enlightenment. And most of all take pride in yourself, of who you have become and will continue to become. Accept yourself for the wonderful, beautiful and positive human being that you are created to be and know that you can in turn, have the awesome power to touch, move and inspire everyone in your life.

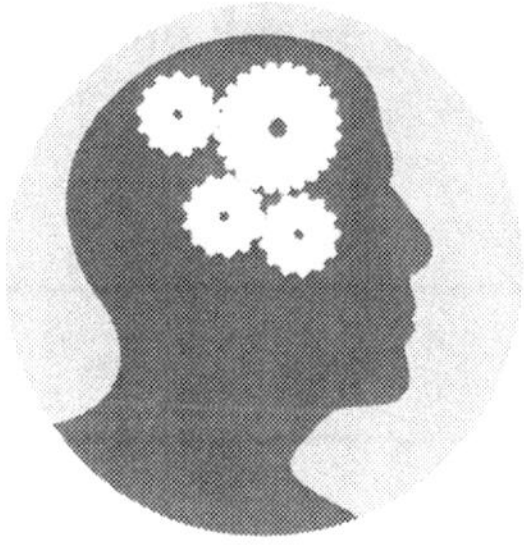

Discovery Exercise:
Step Nine – Walk it Out

Up to this point we have covered nine steps in the "W.A.I.T!" journey. Each step has provided instruction for you to develop and learn new concepts for becoming a "new you". In the exercise below, take a moment to outline your journey using the steps that have been covered:

A **Step One:** Did you take a moment for self reflection? What was revealed?

____

____

____

____

____

____

____

B **Step Two:** What was your quality decisions based on your revelations?

Step Three: What were the new paths that you chose to take?

D **Step Four:** What boundaries were established?

Step Five: What fences did you find yourself putting up to protect yourself in your newly established path?

Step Six: What things were you able to leave in your past?

G. **Step Seven:** What wisdom did you apply in allowing corrections and direction for your newly established path?

____

____

____

____

____

____

____

____

____

____

____

____

H **Step Eight:** What support system was put in place to hold you accountable during this journey?

Step Nine: Where are you with your outlined plans to continue making progress?

REDEFINE, REALIGN
AND
REDESIGN YOUR LIFE
FROM THE
INSIDE OUT

Make a Decision to Stick With It

A Selah Moment

"Character does not examine what you will do tomorrow, but marks what you are doing today."

— S. Yvon Harper

Sticking With It

Finally, let me assure you that as you continue to walk your way through "W.A.I.T!" challenges will arise along the way. However, your response to each new challenge should be positive, take the attitude of "Great, I've been waiting for you." Welcome these challenges with open arms, as they will prove to be an amazing opportunity to test your new found character and behavior. How you respond to these challenges will establish your new identity and give you the opportunity to put everything you have learned to practical use.

Consider the beautiful gem…the diamond. The process of how it becomes one of the world's most sought after gems is exactly the process we each must go through to fine tune our personalities and ways of being. The most important element in the process of becoming a diamond is the pressure that is applied. The very thing that would render weaker materials as useless will cause the diamond to develop into one of the strongest, most beautiful gems known to man. A substance of great worth!

And so it is with the challenges you will face as you walk out your process towards permanent change. The impending challenges will create confidence, tenacity and growth that can only come by applying pressure. So don't back away…embrace the opportunity for richer development and progress will follow. Your victory is in the process!

The uncertainty of these pending challenges was a point of anxiety for the Rich's as well. Several discussion with Sean and Donna centered on concerns expressed about not being successful and conquering their future obstacles. Nonetheless, a thorough review of their individual and collaborative plans helped to assure them they were ready for their "journey".

The General's Plans

Wise people have a plan for their lives. The benefit that "W.A.I.T!" provides is that the plan takes on a written form. What is the advantage and significance of having a written plan? It will help guide you through life's obstacles, challenges and uncertainties by serving as a roadmap to assist you in maneuvering them.

During times of combat, the General in charge will not rely on his memory for the strategic maneuvers needed to win the war. Instead he relies on carefully crafted plans of the battlefield. And similarly you are the "General" in your life's battle to gain permanent change. Your troops are the "W.A.I.T!" tools that have been provided to you that will help you stand firm. Just as a General would be familiar with the enemy he faces, you also need to know your enemy to be successful in your battle. Your pre-established plan will equip you with the ability to stand with confidence and expect victory.

Milestones

Throughout your journey it will be necessary to plan and measure your projected progress against reaching your stated goals. This can best be done by putting milestones in place as a point of reflection. A milestone is a measurement of progress. For example, if your stated goal is to curb your spending habits, a good milestone could be the avoidance of unnecessary purchases in a three week period. A dieter can measure a milestone by reaching the loss of three inches within a given period of time. A person working on interpersonal skills could choose a milestone of having a conversation without raising the tone of their voice inappropriately. All these examples show a measurement of progress towards a stated goal. There cannot be enough said about the importance of using milestones throughout your journey. In fact, without milestones you can waste valuable time by missing necessary steps and opportunities to make possible adjustments. Milestones can also prevent you from repeating harmful mistakes without justification.

Celebrate

Reaching a milestone, should be followed by self acknowledgement and a cause for celebration. Each milestone is a part of the success you are striving to achieve.

Acknowledgment through personal celebration is a significant step. Whether it's the enjoyment of a scoop of your favorite ice cream, a purchase of a new shirt or posting the accomplishment in a prominent place for all who passes by to see. Be sure to celebrate. And remember to accept with much gratitude all the accolades from those who have served as your accountability partners, mentors and friends who supported and value your newly established goals. Their acknowledgement and continued support will provide new zeal for you to continue on towards the new life you desire.

It is important to remember that even if you miss obtaining one of your goals, the fact that you went for it still represents that there has been progress. Keep taking the offensive and consistently review your goals, learning from any obstacles or mistakes. Make the needed adjustment and jump back in with full zeal towards your goal. The bottom line is to keep moving forward at all costs.

Benefits and Rewards

Remember the benefits that pursuing "W.A.I.T!" offers you in creating a permanent change in your life. Freedom from past condemnation, realization of once forbidden dreams and the establishment of a stable foundation for future success is all yours for the taking! In reality only you can identify the immeasurable value that will be added to your present circumstances by applying "W.A.I.T!"'s principles.

The Rich's experienced the ultimate satisfaction of gratification from applying the "W.A.I.T!" system. Their commitment and diligence rewarded them immensely. Not only were they able to reach their initial goal of financial stability, but by applying "W.A.I.T!"'s principles to their individual goals within relationships, careers, and reshaping their personal habits, their marriage and family relationships have also benefited from positive measurable results.

The Rich's discovered that only they could limit the potential successes they could achieve. Now it's up to you to do the same. The choice is yours to either put to use these proven steps to activate the power they hold in your life or set them on a shelf. Either way, know that you have embarked on a journey for permanent change, which will end in the total satisfaction of self accomplishment and victory or in total unresolved regret, because of lack of follow through. I encourage you to persevere...take the journey.

The Last Stand

As I close, let me share with you one final quote that has helped keep my own vision and efforts focused on the positive end results I wanted to achieve.

> *"Therefore take up the whole armor of God, that you may be able to withstand in the evil day, and having done all, stand."*
>
> Ephesians 6:13

As you keep practicing each of the 10 Steps, it will bring you closer to your goal of realizing productive, permanent change in each selected area of your life. Each step is taken by you, through your own efforts. Realize that you will be offered the opportunity along the way to give up or linger in the process. This is why your decision to progress must be sure and steadfast.

The passage quoted above affirms that challenges will happen during your walk, but with the instructions and lessons you have learned in "W.A.I.T!" you now have the necessary armor to withstand these attacks. I strongly suggest that if you have not yet made a decision to pursue permanent change, then now is the time to walk it out! The choice is solely yours.

The question of "What Am I Thinking" is one that only you can answer. If your thoughts are not in line with your stated goals for permanent change, now is the time to align them. Otherwise, the end results will render you ineffective in your life's journey to accomplish all the possibilities that are yours for the taking! Live your life to fullest, choose wisely, and embrace the new you that now has successfully learned to "W.A.I.T!"

Contact the Author

S. Yvon Harper is a certified coach and is available for personal coaching, media interviews, book club moderation and speaking engagements.

Let us know how you're enjoying The WAIT! Book by dropping us an email or giving us a call.

Address:	3189 Princeton Road #201
	Hamilton, OH 45011
Phone:	(513) 341-5912
E-mail:	Contact@TheWaitBook.com

Visit The W.A.I.T! Book website at:

www.TheWaitBook.com

☞ *Find us on* ☜

Join the WAIT! Movement and stay connected
'Like' our Facebook page.

Facebook Fan Page:
www.Facebook.com/TheWaitBook

Follow The Wait Book on Twitter

Twitter Page:
www.Twitter.com/TheWaitBook

Congratulations!

You're now set to begin your personal WAIT! journey to Redefine, Realign and Redesign Your Life from the Inside Out. This is a transformational life changing decision. As such, we have a special gift to support your journey.

Visit the WAIT! Resources page for 2 COMPLEMENTARY tools to assist you in the journey. Come back and visit the WAIT! Resources page regularly as we will update it with additional materials. So register now to gain immediate access. Just scan the QRC or go to the website below.

Don't delay and here's to your success!

www.TheWaitBook.com/Resources

P.S. Registration information is 100% safeguarded and NEVER shared!

CPSIA information can be obtained at www.ICGtesting.com
Printed in the USA
LVOW10s0711240913

353578LV00002B/2/P